NUMBER FIVE
Essays on the American West
sponsored by the
Elma Dill Russell Spencer Foundation

THE GRAVE OF JOHN WESLEY HARDIN

THE GRAVE OF
JOHN WESLEY HARDIN

Three Essays on

Grassroots History

by

C. L. SONNICHSEN

TEXAS A&M UNIVERSITY PRESS

College Station and London

Library of Congress Cataloging in Publication Data

Sonnichsen, Charles Leland, 1901–
    The grave of John Wesley Hardin.

    (Essays on the American West; no. 5)
    Includes bibliographical references.
    1. Frontier and pioneer life—Texas—Addresses,
essays, lectures. 2. Vendetta—Texas—History—Addresses, essays, lectures. 3. Folk-lore—Texas—
Addresses, essays, lectures. 4. Hardin, John Wesley,
1853–1895—Addresses, essays, lectures. 5. Texas—
History—1846–1950—Addresses, essays, lectures.
6. Sonnichsen, Charles Leland, 1901– —Addresses,
essays, lectures. I. Title. II. Series.
F391.S698   976.4   79-7406
ISBN 0-89096-081-X

FIRST EDITION
Manufactured in the United States of America

To the memory of Elmer Spellman and J. R. Webb,
who enriched the life of Texas and encouraged its historians

CONTENTS

PREFACE

THE three essays which follow, published at various times in various periodicals, have two things in common. First, they deal with grassroots history—a thing quite different from formal history as written by academic historians. The first one tells something about what a grassroots historian is and how he works. The second and third are examples of what he does. Second, they are concerned with the feuds of Texas, a subject peculiarly suited to grassroots investigation, one which has occupied me off and on for many years and taken me deep into the heart of Texas and its past.

"Blood on the Typewriter" appeared in somewhat different form under the title "The Grassroots Historian" in *The Southwestern Historical Quarterly* 73 (January, 1970), 381–392; "The Pattern of Texas Feuds" as "The Folklore of Texas Feuds" in *Observations and Reflections on Texas Folklore*, Publications of the Texas Folklore Society No. 37 (Austin: Encino

Press, 1972), pp. 35–47; "The Grave of John Wesley Hardin" in *Password* 22 (Fall, 1977), 91–108. These essays are reprinted with the consent of editors L. Tuffly Ellis, Francis E. Abernethy, and Conrey Bryson.

Thanks are due to several hundred informants who helped in the production of this book and of the five volumes on Texas and New Mexico feuds which preceded it, to the librarians, newspaper editors, archivists, and keepers of family papers who contributed material, counsel, and encouragement, and to the unorganized fraternity of grassroots historians who endeavor to support and cheer each other and sometimes read each other's works.

C. L. SONNICHSEN
Arizona Historical Society
Tucson, Arizona

THE GRAVE OF JOHN WESLEY HARDIN

BLOOD ON THE
TYPEWRITER

HISTORIANS of the American West fall into two general classes: library and grassroots. The library type talks about the westward expansion, the mining frontier, and the Apache campaigns. The grassroots variety investigates local matters, pioneer experiences of all kinds but particularly those that people hesitate to talk about—family feuds, riots, mobs, vigilantes, shootouts, personal encounters. He is interested, first of all, because he is not supposed to know or ask about these things, and there is—or was—some risk involved in gathering the forbidden fruit. Almost as strong a motive is his urge to record a part of history that may be lost unless he gets it down on paper.

He is interested, very often, in other things besides murder. Sometimes he is not interested in murder at all, but merely wishes to chronicle the beginnings of his town or the ramifications of a particular family. Occasionally he specializes in pioneer tools and artifacts or in the progress of religion in his community. But since law and order were often in short supply in early times and men were inclined to right their own wrongs, nine times out of ten he gets involved in violence of some kind and there is, figuratively speaking, blood on his typewriter.

Such a chronicler expects, and gets, little credit for his efforts, and he hesitates to call himself a historian at all. He works in out-of-the-way places, reads country newspapers, prowls about in county courthouses, and spends a lot of time interviewing old men and women. When he appears at conventions of state historical societies, he does so a little self-consciously and speaks to the professionals courteously and respectfully, if at all. He is low man on the historians' totem pole, but he is not as low as he used to be. His numbers are increasing, publishers are more hospitable to him than in former times, and he has a surprising number of readers. It is time somebody spoke up for him, and since I have been a grassroots historian for forty years, I know a good deal about his diurnal and nocturnal habits, what he does and how he does it and what has happened to him during the years I have had him under observation.

Often he does not recognize himself for what he is. He considers himself a harmless eccentric who collects local history as other people collect mustache cups or

Blue Amberola Edison records. I know about this because I was slow myself to get my bearings. As I look back now, however, I can see that at every turn I was digging deeper into those grassroots—and there was blood on *my* typewriter.

I began working at ground level, soon after I came to Texas in 1931, when I heard about the Jaybird-Woodpecker feud which broke out at Richmond, Texas, near Houston, and ended in a riot around the courthouse in 1889. The Jaybirds and the Woodpeckers! Strange and wonderful. Minnesota and Massachusetts, where I was most at home, could offer nothing comparable. I had to know more. So in the summer of 1933 I went to Richmond to see what I could learn. I returned home to El Paso thoroughly infected and started collecting information about the El Paso Salt War of 1877. Then came an old gambler and saloonkeeper named Billy King, who sent me off to the grassroots at Tombstone, Arizona. After that I began learning about Judge Roy Bean, the Law West of the Pecos, and simultaneously kept files going on more Texas vendettas. Since then I have turned out five books on Texas and New Mexico feud situations, one on Brushy Bill Roberts, who said he was Billy the Kid, a study of the contemporary cattleman based almost entirely on interviews (good grassroots material), and a history of the

Mescalero Apaches that cost me many weary hours cornering old Indians who did not wish to talk to me or anybody else. It was all grassroots history. The projects I am working on now are grassroots history. I am hooked, and it is too late for me to reform.

When I began operations, I found that I was a prophet without honor in any country, especially my own. Zane Grey and the romancers were riding high. The skeptical historians of the fifties and sixties were still in high school, and Eastern publishers were politely incredulous when I suggested that somebody might wish to know, for its own sake, the truth about pioneer times. It took me seven years to place my first book. New York publishers wanted more fiction. Regional publishers wanted more scholarship. As late as February 19, 1954, Bernard W. Shir-Cliff of Ballantine Books wrote of one of my manuscripts: "There is a surprising amount of information in the book but very little feeling for individuals. It is almost as if Sonnichsen's main objective has been to get together in one convenient place the source material which other writers might use."

Savoie Lottinville of the University of Oklahoma Press, on the other hand, said in *his* letter of rejection, dated January 25, 1955: ". . . there is not here a long-term historical significance. . . . You wish to tell us a rattling good story of frontier violence, and you've done

it. If you had been writing for purely scholarly pur-
poses, I think you would have used other devices."

I was neither fish nor flesh, and if I had not been
doing exactly what I wanted to do, published or not,
the thirties and forties would have been traumatic
times. As it was, my record was one book, one publisher
for a long time. For the next book I had to find a new
publisher.

My feud material was hardest to handle. When I
suggested to the management of the *Dallas News* that
what I had dug up might make a good newspaper series,
Mr. Ted Dealey, then vice-president, wrote me on
August 21, 1935: "Frankly, we would be afraid to
handle any of this kind of material. There are very
probably descendants of the participants of these feuds
still living in South Texas, and we think it would be
very bad policy on the part of any newspaper to rehash
this ancient trouble."

New York publishers were even more difficult, but
for different reasons. They were not worried about repercussions in the Pure Feud Belt, but they had other
hangups. After *I'll Die Before I'll Run* was actually in
press at Harper's, I found that my picture section—the
product of years of scouting and, in my view, priceless—
would not do at all. "What we would particularly like,"
editor John Fischer wrote me on November 3, 1950,
"are photographs which are not simply the convention-

al studio portraits. . . . A photograph of a hanging, a body in a morgue, or almost anything else that would give us some action and variety would be desirable."

Although Mr. Fischer was a Texan, he had obviously been away too long. I had to tell him that on the Texas frontier lynch mobs did not wait for a photographer and would probably have hanged the picture man along with the horse thief if he offered to snap his shutter—and that there were no morgues out on the lone prairee.

There was also a deep-rooted prejudice in some quarters against anything with shooting in it. It was a natural and understandable feeling. The sensational chapters of frontier history have always attracted yellow journalists, thrill seekers, and romancers. A grassroots historian, be he ever so serious in his pursuit of truth, is guilty by association, or he was a few years ago. Frank Wardlaw of the University of Texas Press commented on April 21, 1955, apropos of a feud manuscript I had sent him: ". . . there has always been a considerable feeling among the members of the Advisory Board that our regional publishing should be entirely outside the tradition of the Wild West and its badmen. Granted that your book is a serious and historically meticulous study of an important aspect of the state's past, it does deal with bad men and thus has at least one strike against it."

That was the way it was in 1935 and 1945 and 1955. By 1965 everything had changed completely. The pulp magazines were all gone. The writers of westerns had been severely weeded out, and some of them had taken to the writing of legitimate history. Some of them had even gone to work. Magazines like *True West* and *Real West* had appeared in response to the universal demand for "fact." University presses, including the University of Texas Press, had abandoned some of their prejudices against feuds, outlaws, and the bad old days in general, and new presses—the Encino Press, the Pemberton Press, the Texian Press, the San Felipe Press, the Palo Verde Press, the Stagecoach Press—were publishing grassroots history. Even the newspapers had given ground. On October 20, 1963, the *Houston Post* initiated a series of articles on feuds and gunfights in the Sunday magazine section. The author was Roy Grimes of Victoria, but I was given credit for "painstaking research."

Today if one of us fails to interest a commercial publisher and has to pay a subsidy press to have his book published, he usually gets his money back, often goes into a second printing, is reviewed in the city newspapers—even in the historical quarterlies—and may be quoted by important historians. As we used to say, he can "hold his head up," even in pretty fast historical company.

This is the day of the grassroots historian if he is ever going to have one. Beginning novelists and short-story writers find it next to impossible to break into print, but good grassroots materials is in demand. Try writing an article on "The Bad Girls of San Diego," or "New Light on the Pleasant Valley War in Arizona," or "The Day Wyatt Earp Was Run out of El Paso" (there is a tradition that he found the town too hot to handle). Somebody will publish you, and may even pay you.

All sorts of subjects interest the grassroots historian, but for most of us who work at this level, the most intriguing years—the years which offer the greatest challenge—are the decades after the Civil War when the law broke down or was not available. In times like these, people find it necessary to make their own law, and they try to do it without publicity. As a result, the records are likely to be few and far between.

These two or three decades were about as bad as they could be (accounting for some of the blood on the historian's typewriter). Organized gangs of thieves preyed on the settlers, and the settlers protected themselves by setting up vigilance committees, locally called "whitecaps" or "mobs," which shot or hanged the desperadoes. When these invokers of self-redress or folk justice went too far and extended their activities to citizens with nothing on their consciences, the victims formed their own groups and "moderated" the Regulators.

The feuds which resulted characterized the 1870's, continued through the 1880's, and even cropped up in the 1890's and the early 1900's. Some are said to throw off sparks even today. There must have been at least a hundred of them, big and little, excluding many a grudge murder, crime of passion, or "difficulty" (the old Texas word for a pitched battle) which never quite developed into a series of revenge killings. Texans fought about anything in those days. There was feuding over race, politics, prohibition, and stock stealing—especially stock stealing. Once ablaze, a feud tended to move out of the rocky hills and mesquite pastures and involve the people in town, including the law officers. It never slowed down by itself but moved on toward extermination of both sides unless an outside agency—Sam Houston or the Texas Rangers—took charge and cooled it off. Small armies marched and countermarched in Shelby County during the war of the Regulators and Moderators. The Sutton-Taylor feud went on for over thirty years.

In such times, when legal redress was not available or not wanted, people went back to the customs under which their Saxon forebears had operated—an eye for

an eye, a life for a life. Revenge was a duty, the death of
one of the enemy was an occasion for loud rejoicing,
and all scruples about the method of killing him van-
ished. Waylaying (sometimes called "laywaying") was
not merely tolerated but strongly recommended, and
everybody knew that the right way to handle it was to
get down behind a bush beside the road, wait till your
target for tonight rode past you, and then fire at the
place where his suspenders crossed, the steadiest part of
a man-horse combination. If you warned him to leave
the country and he didn't go, you liquidated him without compunction and reasoned that he had committed
suicide.

Eventually it was all over, and the survivors followed a new pattern. They walked warily and they kept
their mouths shut. Some of them had heavy burdens on
their consciences and didn't want their deeds discussed,
might even eliminate a man who told what he knew.
Others were afraid the trouble might break out again if
somebody "talked," and sometimes it almost did. There
was also a feeling that if nobody mentioned those awful
things, they might somehow be forgotten or go away.

In spite of the no-talk rule, it took a long time for
the hatreds and guilt feelings engendered by a feud
situation to cool off. Fifty years would be a reasonable
estimate of the time required for the fire to die out,
and even then there would be embers.

The result, historically speaking, was usually a great scarcity of recorded information about these troubles. So carefully were they hushed up that a feud which had upset everybody in one county might be almost unheard of in the county next door.

Obviously a library historian would not be the man to gather the facts about a Texas feud. It takes a specialist, a real grassroots historian, to do it. He has to use every source, likely or unlikely, that he can get to. He not merely reads newspapers and court records; he checks the land records, the church records, and the census reports. He works with tombstones and wills. And everywhere he goes, he tries to get people to talk. He knows they can't be trusted, that they must be forever checked against each other and against the record. But he can't do without them, because they were there. If he finds no way of reconciling or choosing between their stories, he has to tell both versions and let his readers make the choice.

Half the time he is dealing with folklore. His informants pass on the original facts with all the embroideries time and a partisan interest can attach, and he has to try to draw a clear line between fact and fabrication. He knows, better than most historians, that folklore is a branch of history. What people have agreed to believe about the facts is a fact in itself, and sometimes it is much more influential than the reality. Jesse James may possibly have been more interested in booty than in justice, but it made considerable difference in the unfolding of his career that his neighbors thought of him as a crusader against the iniquities of the railroad magnates.

Thus it is that the grassroots historian brings some special skills and some special understanding to his task. He also brings a sense of urgency. He has a limited time in which to work before the night cometh, in which no man can work. Hervey Chesley of Hamilton, Texas, a grassroots specialist himself, commented on this fact in a letter to me dated November 7, 1958:

> Back as far as I remember, you were not supposed to talk about those old feuds and mobs, of course. It just wasn't supposed to be discussed, I guess. Then for a short period of years you could probably have learned something about it when so many had died off that the few remaining did not mind spilling the beans. I just happened to pick up enough from the last survivor of one of those episodes that I don't suppose my life would have been worth four bits in depreciated currency if I had known it way back there and they had known I knew it. Then soon of course practically all of them passed on and all you can pick up now is just a little second-hand stuff and not much of that.

So grassroots history has to be collected, like the manna of the Hebrews, at exactly the right moment, and a researcher is lucky if he does not come too early or too late. The difficulty in timing, however, is over-shadowed by the fear a grassroots historian often feels for the integrity of his own hide. He just might get shot.

From the beginning, I was nervous about the business of feud collecting. It was not easy to knock on doors and ask the gentle ladies who peered out at me about the scandalous doings of their family and friends, and I kept running into bits of folklore and tradition which were anything but reassuring. The last researcher who came to Cuero to investigate the Suttons and the Taylors, I was told, was escorted to the railway station by a committee of townspeople, hustled aboard a train, and told not to return. I had heard the same story closer to my home about a man who had inquired on the streets of Las Cruces, New Mexico, about the trouble between lawyer A. J. Fountain and rancher Oliver Lee. I was prepared to believe that this was standard procedure in the Pure Feud Belt, and I thought it would probably happen to me.

Kindly old Dr. Joseph R. Lay, when I went to see him in Houston, assured me that when the ladies of Richmond got together for a card party, they very carefully avoided all references to Jaybirds and Woodpeckers and allied forms of bird life for fear of starting the trouble all over again. I believed him.

Somewhere else I picked up the idea that neutrals were not allowed in feuding towns, that even strangers passing through had to declare themselves. It seemed to me that this must be true when I heard what happened to a circuit-riding minister who visited Richmond when feeling was running high. This was before Carry Nation had given up Richmond and Texas as a bad job and gone to see what she could do for Kansas. She and her preacher husband were still running the National Hotel, and the circuit rider registered there and was given a room on the second floor. About the time he got his shoes off and started to relax, he heard footsteps on the stairway and responded to an imperative knock on his door. Half a dozen citizens faced him.

"Reverend," said the spokesman, "we're having a feud here. The Jaybirds are fighting the Woodpeckers and we don't allow any neutrals. If you are going to spend any time in Richmond, you'll have to tell us which side you are on, so there won't be any mistakes. Which are you going to be—a Jaybird or a Wood-pecker? We're Jaybirds ourselves."

"Well, I hardly know. I just arrived and don't know a thing about local matters. Could I have till to-morrow to decide?"

"Yes, I guess so. We'll be back in the morning."

They clumped off down the stairs and the preach-er began to breathe a sigh of relief, but before he got it all the way out, he heard another knock on his door, and there were the Woodpeckers, who went through the same routine.

This time, however, the preacher had recovered from his first astonishment and knew what to say. "Gentlemen," he told them, "I am a preacher of the gospel. I came here to save souls, not to get involved in your political troubles. I am neither a jaybird nor a woodpecker, but if I have to be some kind of bird, I am a turkey buzzard and it's ten dollars' fine to shoot me."

A grassroots historian, just learning his business, got no comfort from a story like that, and it was worse when he heard about the toughness of those feuding towns. The old men told how the brakemen on the train from Houston behaved when they approached Hempstead, known then and now as Six-Shooter Junction. They would pass through the coaches intoning, "Hempstead! Hempstead next! Prepare to meet thy God!" And all the passengers would crouch down between the seats and wait for the shooting to start.

They told about two men sitting out in front of the Three Brothers Saloon in Hempstead on a peaceful spring morning, serene and kindly men without a grudge in the world. One of them turned to the other and asked:

"Jim, you got any chewing tobacco?"

"Yes, I do."

"Give me a chaw, will you?"

"Sure. It's in my hip pocket. Reach in there and get it."

Jim would not reach for his hip pocket under any circumstances. If anybody happened to shoot him at that moment, the jury would call it self-defense.

The fact is, none of the things I was afraid of happened to me. Nobody escorted me to a train. Nobody suggested that I ought to mind my own business. All the Woodpeckers left Richmond in 1889 and the survivors of the feud, all Jaybirds, were the soul of kindness and courtesy. I did call on one Woodpecker lady in Houston, but when I explained my business through a screen door, she burst into tears and disappeared into the back rooms of the house. She was not discourteous, however, just unhappy. One prominent Jaybird (the party continued to function until recently) who wanted to know what I was doing asked me to meet him in a Houston hotel lobby. Guileless as I was, I was eager to see him, and as soon as we were settled in a couple of hotel chairs, I began showing him my extracts from the "Richmond Rustlings" column contributed to the *Houston Post* by David Nation, husband of the immortal Carry. David was not accepted in the social life of Richmond and was eventually beaten up and run out of town by a group of young Jaybirds who were displeased by something he said in his column, but he did report on the Richmond parties, and he brought back some wonderful memories to my Jaybird friend. "Why, that's the girl I married," he exclaimed, pointing to a name in a list of guests. And there was peace between us.

So the Jaybirds gave me their blessing, and some of them are still my friends. I think my ignorance and innocence were on my side. I worked for twenty years, off and on, on this incendiary material and had no trouble in Texas, though I ran into some heavy weather in New Mexico which delayed me for two years in publishing *Tularosa: Last of the Frontier West.* If I had known at the beginning what I knew at the end, I probably would have let it alone. But the people I worked with were almost always helpful.

I was never really easy in my mind, however, until I began working on the Johnson-Black-Echols feud, which reached its climax at Coahoma, a village a few miles east of Big Spring, in 1911. Shine Phillips, druggist and sage of Big Spring, introduced me to a senior representative of one of the clans, and we had an interview in the back of the Phillips drug emporium. I explained my objectives, and my new friend listened. He told me what a burden the memory of that old feud had been to him and all the family, how they had tried to lead good Christian lives and serve their community, hoping they could "live it down." He did not object to my telling the story, he said, "if I thought it would do any good," and I went on down to Austin to check the files of the appeals court where the litigation had finally reached an end.

In July, 1945, after I had put everything together and written the story, I did what I always made a practice of doing—I sent a copy of the manuscript to the man who had given me the information. I got a letter back. It said:

Dear Mr. Sonnichsen:

I have read your letter and have shown it to my brothers. We would like to talk to you about your manuscript. Could you meet us at some place between Coahoma and El Paso, say Barstow?

I knew well enough what this meant, and I sent back a soft answer to the effect that if anybody was going to be unhappy about publication of this particular episode, I would give it up. After all, 1911 was not very long ago. Perhaps it was too soon to tell the story.

I got back a touching reply, dated August 5, 1945:

Dear Mr. Sonnichsen:

I received your kind letter a few days ago and note that you are willing to leave out the Coahoma trouble from your book. After I talked with some of Uncle Price's children I found out that it would break their hearts if the story is ever published.

That put a different face on everything. The last thing I wanted to do was to break somebody's heart. So the Coahoma Shootin' story is still unpublished and will probably remain so. But the letter removed the last trace of uneasiness from my soul about what might happen to me personally. I knew at last that if I talked straight and kept my hands in sight, I would probably survive—and I have.

I have felt better, too, as the years have gone by, about the value of grassroots history. I once defined a grassroots historian as a man who spends his time finding out what nobody wants him to know and he would be better off not knowing. I think of him now as a useful member of the great historical orchestra—a second violin or maybe a piccolo player—inconspicuous but needed to complete the harmony. His folk history involves fundamental patterns of human thought and behavior which have their repercussions in the capitals of the world. Gordon Wilson comments on this fact in his book *Passing Institutions*: "There are so many customs connected with every historical event that to know folk habits is almost to know human history, the written, and still more, the unwritten. Our own American History is written much more in the changing customs than hundreds of years of writing can ever record it. When more historians realize that folk movements are the basis of our formal history, then a true history can be written."[1]

[1] Gordon Wilson, *Passing Institutions: A Series of Essays about Things We Used to Know* (Cynthiana, Ky.: privately published, 1943), preface.

Andrew Jackson took his Tennessee roots with him to the White House. Lyndon Johnson took his Texas roots with him when he became president. The historians of the labor movement, of native American music, of farmer cooperatives—all are using grassroots techniques. When it is time to write the history of Students for a Democratic Society, the historian will have to go to the grassroots—the grassroots of Harvard Yard. Everywhere and in every way we are getting back to the people—and that is just what the grassroots historian has been doing all along.

There is still time to find out a little more about the days when our country was in the making, though the earlier chapters are closed. A good grassrooter can still get inside information, for instance, on rumrunning and moonshining during the prohibition era, and men are still around who belonged to the Ku Klux Klan during its revival in the 1920's. At any period it is possible to feel as Pres Lewis does in Eugene Manlove Rhodes' *The Trusty Knaves*, when he says to an observant tenderfoot:

> You have a fine inquiring mind, and you want to remember that in a thousand years or some such, historians will publicly offer their right eye to know what you can see now, at first hand; just as they puzzle and stew and guess about Harold the Saxon, nowadays. . . . Here you are, living in the ancient days and the springtime of the world, with a priceless chance to get the lowdown on how we scramble

through with a certain cheerfulness and something not far removed from decency and make merry with small cause.[2]

But even if there were no connection between grassroots history and larger issues, we grassroots historians have one satisfaction other historians can never share. When we have finished our job, no matter how much we miss, how shallow our thinking, how amateurish our writing, we have done a job nobody can do over. The door which opens for so brief a time closes while we watch it. The last survivor dies before we get into print. For better or for worse, we have done what we could while we could. And we have said the final word. There won't be any more.

[2] Eugene Manlove Rhodes, *The Trusty Knaves* (Boston: Houghton Mifflin Co., 1933), pp. 115–116.

THE PATTERN OF
TEXAS FEUDS

BACK in the early thirties, for reasons which have never been quite clear to me, I became a specialist in the feuds of Texas, and ever since then I have collected vendettas as other people collect duelling pistols or vintage automobiles. I am probably the only one of my kind, for feuds are dangerous and difficult things to deal with, but I have no regrets. I learned a great deal about human history and human nature and made contact with some of the most interesting people one could ever hope to meet, the sons and daughters of the feuding clans of Texas.

First of all, I learned that feuds follow patterns as old as mankind, patterns which we have spent thousands of years trying to get rid of with only indifferent success and which we repeat, step by step, whenever conditions are right. They teach us that in all of us the old primitive instincts are present, just below the surface, ready to take over when we are frightened, abused, or driven beyond the limits of endurance.

Before I attempt to tell what a feud is or isn't, and how it operates, it might be well to look at a sample. There were at least a hundred feuds in Texas in early days, some of them lingering on for as much as thirty years, some involving hundreds of people and dozens of deaths. A typical example would be the terrible outlaw feud north and east of Austin in the seventies and early eighties. The village of McDade was a focal point, and one of several climaxes came in the form of a multiple hanging in 1883.[1]

McDade is now a wide place in the road thirty-eight miles east of Austin at the edge of an area of post oaks and bottomland which is still pretty rough and rugged. A sort of infection center in the early days was the district known as "the Knobs," from three good-sized green hills ten or twelve miles north of McDade. In the shadow of the Knobs was the Blue or Blue Branch community, where terrible deeds were done in the early days and where a man could probably still arrange for a fight if he wanted one badly enough.

As early as 1868 stories appeared in print hinting at bands of horse thieves and desperadoes hanging out in this region.[2] When McDade became a railhead in the

[1] The story of the McDade lynching feud is condensed from "Four on a Limb: The McDade Hangings," in C. L. Sonnichsen, *I'll Die Before I'll Run* (New York: Devin-Adair, 1962; first published by Harper, 1951).

[2] Mrs. Edward C. Garland, *Galveston News*, April 12, 1868.

fall of 1871, boom-town life on a small scale was added to the ordinary perils of existence.[3] The thugs in the thickets increased and multiplied, robbed cotton farmers heading home with their crop money, and rustled cattle and horses by the hundreds. In those days the big cattlemen kept bands of tough cowboys who didn't much care what brands were on the hides of the steers they drove off to Kansas. The little cattlemen got even by picking up what the big fellows didn't take care of. Such small-time larceny was something frontier settlers had to expect. What could not be shrugged off was the wholesale stealing of the "Gang."

This Gang—members were sometimes called Notchcutters because they lived out in the post oaks, mostly—was a mysterious organization which went about its business with great caution and cleverness. Its members were loyal and secretive to the death and thought nothing of committing perjury or murder to protect their brothers in crime.

Following the familiar pattern, a counter organization began to take shape in the middle seventies. In 1874 several supposed criminals were found hanging from trees, and the Gang retaliated whenever it could, bushwhacking horsemen and sending farmers home dead in the bottoms of their ox wagons.

[3] *Flake's Semi-Weekly Bulletin* (Houston) October 4, 1871.

The biggest cattlemen in the region were soon drawn in. Twenty miles or so from McDade lived the Olive family—James Olive and his sons Jay, John, Ira, and Prentice. The latter, called "Print" Olive, was known all over the cattle country in later years.[4] In 1876 he was a tough Texas cattleman who was obviously serious when he said that he and his men "would kill anyone they found skinning their cattle or riding their horses."[5]

On March 22, 1876, the first result of this policy appeared when two men named Turner and Crow were left dead on the prairie beside the Olive beeves they had been skinning. Their bodies were wrapped in the green hides as a warning to anybody who might be interested.[6]

A good deal of skirmishing and nightriding followed, culminating on August 1, 1876, in a night attack on a concentration of Olive men camped in the yard of one of their ranch houses. Jay Olive died of

[4] Mari Sandoz in *The Cattlemen* (New York: Hastings House, 1958), pp. 68–76, gives a full though fictionalized and undocumented account of the Olives in Texas and Nebraska. Harry E. Chrisman in the Denver Westerners *Roundup* 17 (June, 1961), 13–15, defends the brothers against the charge of extreme brutality.

[5] *Austin Weekly Statesman*, August 10, 1876.

[6] Ibid., March 30, July 27, August 18, 1876; Judge C. W. Webb, Elgin, Texas, June 6, 1943, interview; Tom Elder, McDade, Texas, June 26, 1943, interview.

wounds received in this fight, and several others were
hurt. The Olives retaliated and as a result were brought
to trial at Georgetown. The situation was very tense as
the Olive supporters camped on one side of town and
the opposition on the other, scaring unsuspecting tra-
velers and getting ready for civil war. The Olives were
acquitted, however, without a fight, and Print soon
after moved his family and his herds to Nebraska and
Kansas, where he made more history.[7]

Still the robbing and murdering went on. Men
were found hanging in the woods, their own stake ropes
around their necks. Texas newspapers complained that
crime was rampant and that "there have been more
men killed in Texas in the last year than she lost during
the late war."[8] The McDade region was regarded as
about the hottest spot anywhere.

Again outlaw alliance was met by a counter organization—perhaps a revival of the vigilante group of
1874. Newspapers reported that an initiation fee was
charged and that the money was used to run down
thieves who stole from the members.[9] Of course both

[7] Mari Sandoz in *The Cattleman* follows Nebraska tradition in giving the Olives the worst of it. Harry E. Chrisman in
The Ladder of Rivers (Denver: Sage Books, 1962) is generally
favorable to them.

[8] *Austin Weekly Statesman*, April 25, 1876.

[9] *Western Chronicle* (Sutherland Springs, Texas), May 17,
1878.

sides kept their business carefully under cover, but that such an organization existed is proved by what happened next—the multiple hanging of 1877 at the Knobs.

At this time Pat Earhart, a man a little out of place in this frontier world, was living out at Blue. He had better clothes and manners than his neighbors, some education, and considerable musical talent. He ran a singing school and played the fiddle for the dances frequently held at his house.[10] Whenever that fiddle began to squeak, all the young bucks in the neighborhood were sure to be there, no matter which side they were on.

The most famous of all Earhart's dances was in full swing on June 27, 1877, when several masked members of the vigilante organization appeared at the front and back doors and told Pat to call out the names of five men who were wanted. Wade Alsup, John Kuykendall, Young Floyd, and Beck Scott responded. The fifth man managed somehow to make himself scarce and is said to be running yet.[11]

The four men had arms enough to fight a battle, but their guns were stacked in the lean-to. Besides, they did not seem to realize what was happening. Beck Scott,

[10] Tom Elder, interview.
[11] Helen Rummel, "When Eleven Were Lynched," *Austin Daily Statesman*, June 29, 1928.

who was dancing with Fanny Alsup when his name was called, borrowed her fan, remarking, "It will be hot as hell before we get to Giddings." He thought he was being arrested and taken to the county seat. Wade Alsup caught on faster. "You won't need no fan where we're going," he said.[12]

It was about two o'clock in the morning when this happened. The masked men took their prisoners out into the darkness and hanged them to a tree five hundred yards from the house—four on a limb.[13]

For a while the shock of this violent deed worked minor miracles. Jim Floyd, a brother of one of the victims, left the country, got religion, and became a preacher. Others may have been frightened into a similar change of heart. But mostly the sinners went on sinning, and the righteous continued to lose their lives and their money. By 1883 the time was ripe for another explosion. Several people had been killed, including a harmless old storekeeper and a popular deputy sheriff.[14] The citizens had had enough.

On December 7 two hundred of them assembled

[12] Tom Elder, interview.

[13] *Austin Daily Statesman*, June 29, June 4, 1877; Jeptha Billingsley, assisted by Mrs. Emma S. Webb, "McDade Lynchings Fifty Years Ago Remembered," *Elgin Courier*, June 25, 1953.

[14] J. J. Sapp, Bastrop, Texas, June 13, 1943, interview; *Bastrop Advertiser*, November 25, 1883; *Galveston News*, November 25, December 4, 1883.

openly in the little wooden church at the east end of
McDade (the only one in town) to talk about a little
righteous hanging. Even now nobody will tell who was
there, though all the oldtimers could mention names. I
myself have never tried to identify a single participant.
There are some things I just don't want to know. It is
said, however, that the assembly went very thoroughly
into the list of men who would have to be got rid of before there could be peace and order in the country, and
at least one of those present heard the name of a near
relative called out and confirmed while he sat tight,
unable to do a thing about it.[15]

The *Galveston News* carried a story about the
meeting the next day. It mentioned no names but said
the object of the participants was to "assist the officers
of the law" and described them as "the very best citizens."[16]

On Christmas Eve, 1883, the meeting bore fruit. A
noisy bunch had assembled in the Nash brothers' Rock
Saloon at McDade. Among them were several members
of the Notchcutters—the old Gang. About seven-thirty
a group of masked men quietly entered the front door.
There were more outside, somewhere between forty
and eighty, as the story has been handed down. They

[15] Mrs. C. W. Webb, notes of an interview with Sam Sanders, Elgin, Texas, August 8, 1944; J. J. Sapp, interview.
[16] *Galveston News*, December 9, 1883.

never said a word, but each one had a Winchester in the crook of his arm, and they nudged three men—two Mc-Lemores and Henry Pfeiffer—out of the saloon with those gun barrels. The McLemores are said to have been under indictment for cattle theft. Pfeiffer was taken, they say, because he recognized one of the vigilantes in spite of his mask and called his name aloud.[17]

Another man almost went along, a young fellow from Georgia who had come out to see if the West was as wicked as he had been led to believe. Supposing the men were going to a Christmas Eve dance at the Knobs, he trailed along outdoors but was shoved back by the men with rifles. When he found out next day what sort of party he had almost joined, he was so sick he had to go to bed.[18]

The three victims were taken a mile north of town and hanged from a blackjack tree.

The last killings in the feud took place at McDade the next day, Christmas, 1883. Three Beatty boys—Jack, Heywood, and Az—with their kinfolks Byrd Hasley, Robert Stevens, and Charley Goodman, rode in during the morning to do some shopping. They had not heard of the events of the night before but soon found out. Some of them became very much excited when they were told that Heywood Beatty's name had

[17] J. J. Sapp, interview.
[18] General W. D. Cope, Austin, July 4, 1944, interview.

been called by the vigilantes in the Rock Saloon. They proceeded to call two men to account, local merchants named George Milton and Tom Bishop. The result was a terrific gunfight in the main street of McDade which resulted in the death of Az and Jack Beatty and the accidental killing of an innocent bystander named Willie Griffin.[19] Nineteen-year-old Heywood Beatty put up a heroic fight and escaped through the pastures, marked by bullets in seventeen places.[20]

That was the end of the feud. According to legend another mass meeting was held in McDade at this time, and a list of objectionable people was drawn up. A local doctor was selected as spokesman; he made the rounds, giving the proscribed men ten days to wind up their affairs.[21] Heywood Beatty was one who left. He went to ranching out in the plains country near Weatherford and did not come back for many years. When he did return to settle up some business, he would not reenter the town. "Boys," he said, "I'm out of trouble now and I want to stay out. I won't go in there." And he didn't.[22]

Using the McDade affair as a fairly representative

[19] Billingsley, "McDade Lynchings"; *Bastrop Advertiser,* January 3, 1884; Tom Elder, interview; Dr. G. T. King, Elgin, June 13, 1943, interview. Testimony by Bishop and others was recorded in the *Bastrop Advertiser,* January 16, 1884.

[20] Tom Elder, interview.

[21] Mrs. C. W. Webb, notes of interview with Sam Sanders.

[22] T. U. Taylor, "In and around Old McDade," *Frontier Times,* May, 1939.

example of the Texas variety of feud, I can begin to outline some of the things I have learned about the folklore of the subject.

In the first place there is a set of ideas which might be called *false folklore* which have to be got out of the way at the start. These are the ideas which pop into everybody's mind automatically when somebody says the word *feud.* If these notions have a father, his name is John Fox, Jr., whose *Trail of the Lonesome Pine, A Cumberland Vendetta,* and other works were once widely read. From him, or from the folklore on which he drew, we have come to take it for granted (1) that a feud is strictly a family affair, (2) that it flourishes exclusively among hillbilly and backwoods families, and (3) that it starts from something trivial, like a dispute over a stray cow or a razorback hog.

The McDade feud shows the proportion of truth in these conceptions. First, it was a faction rather than a family affair. As was always the case, family and clan loyalties came into the picture, but they were by no means the most important element in the pattern. This was the situation more often than not in the history of Texas feuds. Long and bloody wars have been fought between Southerners and Yankee sympathizers, between racial groups with Anglo-Saxon "Americans" on one side and Mexicans or Germans on the others, between political factions such as the "Reds" and "Blues"

in the lower Rio Grande valley, between Prohibition-
ists and Wets. There was even a feud at Waco, the Bap-
tist stronghold, between earnest church people and a
group of Doubting Thomases led by the notorious
Brann the Iconoclast.[23] After the feud started, the clans
always gathered, but something besides family matters
usually triggered the first shot.

The McDade feud shows also that feudists are not
always backwoodsmen or mountain boys. It is true that
the Notchcutters were at home in rough country and
were not people of high culture, but better citizens
were also involved. When two hundred of the "best
people" gather in the village church to take the law into their own hands, the trouble is no longer an example
of backwoods brutality.

Finally there is the matter of the trivial cause. At
McDade fifteen years of intolerable persecution by a
secret and secure gang of thieves and murderers was
certainly a major grievance. The old notions, however,
are hard to dislodge. The Darnells and the Watsons,
according to Mark Twain in *Huckleberry Finn*, had
long since forgotten the cause of their quarrel. ". . .
some says it was about a horse or a cow—anyway it was

[23] See Charles Carver, *Brann and the Iconoclast* (Austin:
University of Texas Press, 1957), pp. 154–167, and C. L. Sonnichsen, *I'll Die Before I'll Run* (New York: Devin-Adair,
1962), pp. 285–287, for details.

a little matter." T. D. Clark, leading Kentucky historian, serves it up again. "Trifling matters" such as "live-
stock, women, politics, and thievery have been the most
common sources of strife."[24] One wonders why Mr.
Clark classifies\women and politics as "trifling matters."

What, then, is a feud, and how does it work? In
Texas the definition has to be simple and inclusive:
Any prolonged quarrel between families or factions in-
volving blood vengeance.

Feuds were not necessarily outbreaks of lawlessness. Feud law—an eye for an eye—was the first criminal
code evolved by mankind, and many millenia were
needed to make murder a crime against the state instead of against an individual or a family. Like almost
every other case on record in the Southwest, the Mc-
Dade feud shows that intolerable conditions precede
the outbreak and such troubles occur only when the
civil government is not able to provide justice. It then
becomes necessary to return to an earlier law. What we
get is called folk justice.

H. H. Bancroft in his *Popular Tribunals* contends
that a vigilance committee aims to "assist the law" and
that its action springs from a belief in "the right of the
governed at all times to instant and arbitrary control

---

[24] Mark Twain, *The Adventures of Huckleberry Finn*
(New York: Heritage Press, 1940); T. D. Clark writing on Kentucky feuds in the *Dictionary of American History*.

of the government." This, he maintains, is not lawlessness.[25]

The word most often used for the folk concept at work here is *self-redress*—a belief in righting one's own wrongs, law or no law. Plenty of people today feel that under certain special conditions, any man who is a man will go into action with fists or forty-five. Southern gentlemen have traditionally held to this belief, and since a high percentage of Texas pioneers were Southerners, their ideas about self-redress, combined with frontier notions of folk justice, gave them a double reason for taking the law into their own hands.

The situation was made more inflammable, of course, because everybody in Texas, including little boys and preachers, carried firearms and used them habitually to kill game and sometimes Indians.

Given, then, a pyramid of intolerable situations and a habit of self-redress, feuds are the natural outcome. They are the result of two sets of compulsions: on the one hand the stimuli which prod the feudist into action; on the other, the taboos which he dare not violate.

The first of the compulsions is the duty of revenge. The traditional customs and beliefs by which a man lives compel him to exact blood for blood. When it

[25] H. H. Bancroft, *Popular Tribunals*, 2 vols., in *Works*, 39 vols. (San Francisco: History Company, 1887), vol. 36, p. 10.

came to feuding, the Texas town or family was truly a folk. John Wesley Hardin was involved in his youth in the notorious Sutton-Taylor feud. The Taylors were his relatives by marriage. "He could not have held up his head in the county if he hadn't taken it up," one of his supporters once assured me. Half a dozen stories could be told of vows of revenge taken over the body of a murdered father or brother, vows which drew blood every time.

In such situations it was hard for anybody to remain neutral. A man who was strong enough and popular enough could do it, but usually a would-be noncombatant had to pack up and leave the country. He was not necessarily condemned for doing so. A witness, an innocent bystander, and sometimes even a close relative of the principals could run and still keep some of his credit. Tom Elder was a fourteen-year-old boy when he stood on the store gallery at McDade during the final battle on Christmas Day, 1883. He knew he would be called as a witness and maybe get himself into more trouble. He went home as fast as he could, packed up, and pulled out for the Panhandle. He did not come back for sixteen years. "And I didn't get any letters, either," he told me when I interviewed him. He had no feeling that he had done wrong in leaving. He was just playing it safe.

The second compulsion which motivates the feudist is the need to fight fire with fire. After a couple of revenge killings, all scruples are abandoned. The other side has no conception of honor; our side can't risk giving them an advantage. And pretty soon both factions are shooting from the roadside, surrounding houses at daybreak, taking prisoners out of the jail for midnight hangings, and killing each other like wild animals.

"I don't like that shooting from behind a bush. Why didn't you step into the road?" Colonel Grangerford asked his boy Buck, as Huck Finn tells it. "The Shepherdsons don't, Father. They always take advantage," Buck replied. And the old man made no more objections.[26]

It is only a "scorched earth" policy when one side burns the other out in the dead of winter—one way of getting rid of a dangerous enemy. When a vigilance committee gives a man three days to leave the country and shoots him when he overstays his limit, it is his own fault. When a band of executioners rides off, whooping and singing, after cleaning out a nest of the opposition, there is nothing disgraceful in their mirth. If you had eliminated a nest of rattlesnakes which were threatening you and yours, you would feel like celebrating too.

These characteristic behavior patterns help to explain why a feud cannot be settled by agreement.

[26] Samuel L. Clemens, *The Adventures of Huckleberry Finn* (New York: Heritage Press, 1940), p. 134.

Truces have been arranged more than once in Texas. They last anywhere from fifteen minutes to a few days. Neither side trusts the other, and the agreements are just scraps of paper.

Naturally, then, a feud has no brakes. It grows worse and worse until one side is eliminated or a higher authority steps in and imposes peace.

How much do the women of the group have to do with all this? Plenty! Women seem to be better natural haters than men. More than once in the history of Texas feuds it was a woman who handed her man a shotgun with a significant look. Before the great riot at Richmond in the fall of 1889, the women of the Jaybird faction appeared on the streets with small bags of sand which they handed to men who might be lacking in "grit."[27] After the shooting is over, it is the women who labor most vigorously to keep the old resentments alive. Fifty years after the end of the feud between the Staffords and the Townsends at Columbus, a woman who had been involved was riding in an automobile with a friend of mine. He stopped to pick up another passenger. "If she gets in, I get out," said the first woman. "We don't ride in the same car with those people."

The men, of course, did the actual fighting, and it is always a man who emerges as the epic hero of the

[27] *Galveston News*, August 19, 1889.

feud. The Heroic Age comes again when a feud breaks out, and the leader who can outwit or outfight the opposition becomes a superhuman figure, a Bill Mitchell, a Scott Cooley, a John Wesley Hardin, regarded by lesser mortals with awe. Stories circulate about him, ballads are sung, and his stature increases as he is given credit for exploits he never performed. As Ash Upson said of Billy the Kid, the deeds of "meaner villains" are attributed to him and he becomes, to a greater or less degree, a folk hero.

The taboos or prohibitions in feud lore were as important as the compulsions. A man lost caste, and sometimes his life, if he violated one. First was the rule against "talking." People learned not to open their mouths at all, and they were right in keeping still. I know of at least one feud that was started by talebearers who went back and forth between the two camps. And countless killings and enmities were caused by an injudicious word dropped at the wrong time. Even after half a century the people on the inside hate to tell what they know. When they do, they usually demand and get a promise that they will not be quoted.

The wisdom of this attitude appears clearly in a story about the McDade feud. Pete Allen, bushwhacked early in the trouble, was found dead in the road with the print of a boot heel in his face. Twenty years afterward some of his friends or kinsfolk started speculating about who did it and made up their minds that they could fix the blame. The next step was to try to get even. One night somebody roped at the man they suspected and nearly got him—the rope bounced off his shoulder. Before the would-be avenger could try again, another man confessed on his death bed that he was the one who had stomped Pete Allen's face. Too much talk had nearly brought on more trouble.[28]

The great taboo was against what we now call fraternizing. Our side must have no truck with those low criminals on the other side. And that brings Romeo and Juliet into the picture. The forbidden association becomes a temptation, and some dark night there will be an elopement. I know of three cases of intermarriage —a low percentage but an interesting one. I know also of women who spoiled a good deal of fun for their daughters by worrying lest every new boyfriend might be a connection of the traditional enemy.

A characteristic legend is the "whodunit." After any great killing, somebody goes to trial, but gossip always says he was taking the rap for somebody else. In 1905, for instance, a feud flared up at Hempstead over the prohibition issue. A young man named Roland Brown went to trial for killing Congressman John Pinckney in the "courthouse tragedy." But those in the know say that a group of men was posted in the jury

[28] Tom Elder, interview.

room in a sort of tower at one corner of the building and that they actually fired the fatal shots.

Another familiar question is, "Did he really die?" If the man was a powerful and dangerous leader, there was always a suspicion that a log or a sack of sand was in the coffin instead of the body. A small feud flared up at Richmond after the Jaybirds and the Woodpeckers had settled their differences in which one of the Mitchell family was involved. He moved up to the northern part of the county, where he eventually died of pneumonia. They brought him back to Dr. Gibson's house near Richmond for the funeral, and all of Dr. Gibson's family saw that he was really buried. The other party, unconvinced, used to ask the Gibsons (who were related to both sides) if they were sure that a log had not replaced the body in that coffin. Years later, when it became necessary to move Mitchell's body. It was found that somebody had already opened the coffin, just to make sure.

Only a few humorous stories have been handed down as part of the annals of Texas feuds—they were nothing to laugh about as a rule. There is the legend of the young Taylor who had part of his cheek and jaw shot away in a brush with the Suttons. "Is there anything I can do for you?" one of his friends asked.

"Well, I *would* like a drink of water," said the wounded man, "but I haven't the face to ask for it."

That is pretty much the pattern of Texas feuds.

There was only one big one before 1865, the **War of the Regulators** and Moderators in the 1840's. **The** disturbances which followed the Civil War, however, provided a good breeding ground, and feuding flourished through the sixties and seventies. In the eighties the Texas Rangers brought self-redress and mob rule under control, but there was a curious revival of feuding in the nineties—small but vicious outbreaks which were hard to put down. Since 1900 only occasional disturbances of this type have occured, but they *have* occurred and may be expected to recur every now and then. And why not? The last thing a people gets rid of is its equipment of folklore. And feuds are folklore in action. Grassroots historians know, as conventional historians sometimes do not, that political and social history is solidly grounded on ingrained notions of what a man ought to do and when he ought to do it.

THE GRAVE OF
JOHN WESLEY HARDIN

EARLY in the afternoon on September 29, 1965, I
picked up Walter E. Narzinsky at the Pioneer Monument Company on Alameda Avenue in El Paso, Texas,
and drove him out to Concordia Cemetery, where he
had just finished installing a granite-and-bronze marker
on the grave of John Wesley Hardin. I was acting as
official inspector for the Hardin family.

We drove north through Five Points and out Yan-
dell Avenue to a gate in the north wall leading into a
bleak and barren portion of the old graveyard—a section which had been occupied for the best part of a
century and abandoned for many years. It was a city of
the forgotten dead. A few battered headstones rose up
here and there, but no mounds or monuments showed
where most of the inhabitants were resting or who they
were. The place was kept clear of weeds, but otherwise
the desert had reclaimed it. For seventy years Texas'
number-one gunman had been lying there, his grave

lost and unremembered. Now his memorial was in place. I carried a check for $102, signed by E. D. Spellman of Burnet, Texas, Hardin's grandson-in-law, who was acting for the grandchildren and great-grandchildren. I was to hand it over to Walter Narzinsky if the work was done according to specifications.[1]

It was the end of twenty years of frustration. Marking a grave ought not to be a major undertaking, but this one resisted all efforts. John Wesley Hardin, dead and buried, made almost as much trouble for his friends and relatives who wanted that marker placed as he had for carpetbaggers, gamblers, and assorted gunmen during his life. He was a legend in his own day. He is a legend now. And the last chapter in his legend is the story of that monument, for which Mr. Narzinsky was paid $102 (his work was quite satisfactory) on that brisk but sunny afternoon in September, 1965.

Had Hardin been an ordinary man, installing his marker would have presented no difficulties, but he was not ordinary, living or dead. In his autobiography[2] he lists forty victims who went down before his six-shooters (he does not say how many of them recovered), a rec-

---

[1] C. L. Sonnichsen, Hardin file, contains correspondence noted hereafter and records of interviews along with accounts of episodes described, usually written down the day they occurred.

[2] John Wesley Hardin, *The Life of John Wesley Hardin, from the Original Manuscript, as Written by Himself* (Seguin, Texas: Smith and Moore, 1896).

ord unapproached by any other Western pistoleer. He was not, however, just a handy man with a gun with only an educated trigger finger to give him status. He was, and continues to be, one of the most enigmatic characters of our heroic age—a gentleman in manners and appearance, a Southerner of good family background, intelligent and polite, a professing Christian who could and did teach Sunday school and tried to instill the highest ideals in his children. And yet he was always in the worst kind of trouble, always involved in shooting and gambling scrapes, always on the dodge until the law caught up with him and sent him to prison, and in worse trouble when he got out.

Was he a victim of the bad times after the Civil War? Was he a frontier Dr. Jekyll and Mr. Hyde? Did the death of his brother, hanged by a lynch mob at Comanche, Texas, change him for the worse? Was it the death of his wife while he was serving his time, or his failure in his first fumblings for respectability after he got out? Did any or all of these things alter him and bring him to a bad end? It is still impossible to say, but historians and novelists in about a hundred books keep stirring his dust and probing his psychology. Glendon Swarthout won a Spur Award from the Western Writers of America in 1976 for giving the familiar story a new twist in *The Shootist*.[3] Other versions no doubt

[3] Glendon Swarthout, *The Shootist* (Garden City: Doubleday, 1975), also a successful motion picture.

await us in the years to come, but perhaps nobody will ever understand what lies under the concrete-granite-and-bronze monument which has identified Hardin's grave since September 29, 1965.

Part of the answer may lie in the mixed heritage he received from his father and mother. Keeping this possibility in mind, one has to go back to pre–Civil War days, when twenty-two-year-old James Gipson Hardin (John Wesley's father) received his license to preach and became a circuit-riding Methodist minister based at Tyler, Texas. Among the churches he served was one at Corsicana. The only family in town with a house suitable for the entertainment of visiting clergymen belonged to Dr. William Dixon, and Dixon had an attractive daughter. The inevitable happened, and young Mr. Hardin asked for Mary Elizabeth's hand.

"And have her starve!" thundered her father. "No, you can't have her!"

Hardin came from sturdy stock himself, however, and he persisted. Eventually matters came to a head, and a meeting was held in the Dixon parlor attended by one brother-in-law who was a doctor, two brothers who were doctors, and one brother who was a rancher. Mr. Hardin presented his case, discussion followed, and (according to family tradition) a vote was actually taken. The verdict was favorable, and as a result John Wesley Hardin, second child of James and Mary Elizabeth, was born at Bonham, Texas, on May 26, 1853.[4]

The family was poor but proud. James Hardin did not stay in the full-time ministry. He suffered (again according to family tradition) from the effects of a severe case of whooping cough contracted in childhood, and even when he was grown he would sometimes sound as if he were whooping, especially when he was excited or emotional. When he preached, and particularly when he prayed, he whooped mightily before the Lord. So he gave up the pulpit and took to schoolteaching and the law, neither of which was very profitable. He remained an earnest Christian gentleman, however, and tried to bring up his five children in the paths of righteousness.

His son John Wesley thus combined within himself the widely different temperaments of two interesting Texas families. The Dixons were Southern aristocracy, Texas style—proud, touchy, quick-tempered, sometimes violent. They would not back off from anything or anybody. They carried pistols, like everybody else in that time and place, and would shoot if necessary. In the troubled times after the Civil War, they and their many relatives were often embroiled with carpetbaggers and Yankee soldiers and ex-slaves. Half of Wes (as he was usually called—his mother called him

---

[4] Mrs. Mattie Hardin Smith (JWH's sister), Fort Worth, Texas, June 17, 1944, interview.

Johnny) belonged to the Dixons, and that half kept him in trouble. The other half belonged to the Hardins, giving him his high ideals of personal conduct and his sometimes ostentatious piety. The two halves were held together by an unshakable conviction that every act of his life, including the killing of other men, was necessary and right and done on principle. He was not a split personality, but all his life he was torn between the two warring halves of his nature.

It was a life of guilt and trouble. As his family tells it, his first escapade occurred when his father sent him with some legal papers to his Uncle Barnett Hardin, who lived at Bonham in a big white house with columns, as became a gentleman farmer.[5] When the papers were safely in Uncle Barnett's hands, Wes and one of his cousins wanted to have some fun. After they were supposedly in bed, they went out through the window and proceeded to the black section of town, where a wrestling or boxing match was going on. Wes, always "active," decided to take a hand. He threw the local black boy and then threw him again. The boy said, "No bird ever flew so high I couldn't bring him down. I'll get you tomorrow."

The next day a meeting occurred. Both boys had guns, but Wes was quicker. Uncle Barnett gave him a

[5] "Hardin Home Torn Down," *El Paso Times*, July 11, 1965.

gold piece, sent him back to his father, and advised him, "Do what he says." The elder Hardin had always said he didn't want his sons to run if they got in trouble, but this time he knew that flight was necessary. It would mean a hanging if Wes were caught, so he sent the boy to his relatives at Corsicana. They got him a job teaching school, and he held it for three months. Then he was in trouble again, and once more he had to run.[6] For the next ten years he was always on the move, always in danger from the state police and the relatives of his enemies, always shooting it out with somebody. He had nerve and luck along with unbelievable quickness with a forty-five, and the list of his victims grew longer. He must have kept some sort of tally, perhaps a newspaper clipping file or a diary, or both, for when he wrote his autobiography (finished at El Paso in 1895), he was able to put down names and places in impressive detail.

As blood flowed and men died, however, he never once seems to have felt shame or grief or remorse. The victims, he believed, brought their fate on themselves, and often he viewed his acts in the light of public service. "The best people said I did a good thing," he said of a killing which climaxed a disagreement over gambling, and he added gratuitously: "Reader, you see what drink and passion will do. If you wish to be successful

[6] Mrs. Mattie Smith, interview.

in life, be temperate and control your passions. If you don't, ruin and death is the inevitable result."[7] It does not seem to have occurred to him that this advice could apply also to John Wesley Hardin.

His luck ran out at Comanche, Texas, in 1877. On May 26, backed by his cousins Bill Dixon and James Taylor, he shot and killed Charles Webb, a deputy sheriff of Brown County. He got away and fled to Florida, but his brother Joe, who lived at Comanche, was hanged by a mob of indignant citizens. Eventually Wes was captured, brought back to Texas, and sent to the Huntsville penitentiary, where he spent fifteen years.[8]

Some of those years were used constructively. He says he studied law and theology and was superintendent of the prison Sunday school. After a rebellious beginning, he became a model prisoner and looked forward to leading a better and happier life on his release. His letters to his family have been preserved, and they epitomize one side of his character. To his son John, Jr., he wrote on July 3, 1887:

Now my son your father's affection for you has not decreased with the advance of years but has rather grown brighter & brighter his love for you is as high as the thoughts of man, & they reach the heaven. I have no jewels to send you my boy to adorn and to deck your shapely form

---

[7] Hardin, *Autobiography*, p. 11.

[8] *Galveston News*, September 20, October 7, 1877; Mollie M. Godbold, "Comanche and the Hardin Gang," *Southwestern Historical Quarterly* 68 (July, 1963), 55–57.

but I wish to speak to you of principles which if you ob-
serve and cling to them will be of far more value. . . . Truth,
my son, is a rare and precious gem. . . . Justice is a gem
rich & rare a full brother to truth. . . . Now my son there is
but one way to protect the character, protect wealth, your
possessions, & that is by a strict adherence to truth & justice.

Such conduct, he promised, would win for any boy "the
respect and admiration of all who know him."[9]

That his children were moved by such high-flown
admonition is doubtful. After so many years in prison
Wes was a stranger in his own household, and his voice
was a voice from far away. To make matters worse, his
wife Jane fell sick and died less than a year before his
time was up, destroying his hope for a united family
after his release. He did not despair, however. He had
actually studied hard and learned a good deal of law
during his confinement. He was allowed to leave the
prison to take his bar examinations, and his close relatives say that he placed highest in a group of seventy
candidates. When at last the prison gates opened in
February, 1894, the governor gave him a full pardon.
Hoping for the best, he settled in the town of Gonzales,
where he had many friends, sent for his children, hung
out his shingle, and tried to become a part of the community.[10]

[9] John Wesley Hardin to John Wesley Hardin, Jr., letter
in possession of C. L. Sonnichsen.
[10] Lewis Nordyke, *John Wesley Hardin, Texas Gunman*
(New York: William Morrow, 1957), pp. 241–255; Mrs. Mattie
Smith, interview.

He was frustrated on every side. His children were not at ease with him or with his ideas, and there was friction. He decided to run for the office of sheriff, hoping thereby to improve his standing in the community, and found himself involved in a bitter broil with Major W. E. Jones, the incumbent. Defeated at the polls, he left his children with friends and rode west to Junction, a small county-seat town in the brush country west of Austin, where there was a nest of Hardin relatives. There, in December, 1894, he opened a law office. One month later he married Callie Lewis, still in her teens and unprepared for marriage. Only a few hours after the wedding she left him and refused to see him again. Nobody knows what happened, but Wes knew he would have to move on. While he was wondering what to do, an invitation reached him from "Killin' Jim" Miller, his cousin by marriage, to bring his legal talents to a trial that was about to begin in El Paso, 450 miles to the west. Miller had twice been too slow on the draw in a feud he was having with ex-sheriff Bud Frazer of Pecos and was suing Frazer for assault with intent to murder.[11] Would Cousin Wes assist? Cousin Wes would. And on April 1, 1895, he arrived in the little border town which would be his home for the last four

[11] C. L. Sonnichsen, "A Gentleman from Pecos," in *Ten Texas Feuds* (Albuquerque: University of New Mexico Press, 1951, 1971), pp. 200–209.

and a half months of his life, and where he lies buried today under a marker which is the real subject of this essay.

It was now sixteen years since Hardin had sent the citizens of a Texas town hunting for cover, but his fame was undiminished. As he journeyed westward, people gathered to shake his hand and look at him and speculate among themselves about his nerve and his speed. Wes took it all calmly. He was used to hero worship. In his autobiography he says that on his journey under arrest from Alabama in 1879 people crowded to see him. "One man named Roe actually rode from Memphis to Texarkana to see me. . . . 'Why,' he said, 'there is nothing bad in your face. Your life has been misrepresented to me. Here is $10. Take it from a sympathizer.' "[12]

It was almost the same in 1895. Wes was well dressed, handsome, courtly in his manners, still ready to pray or to fight, still sure of his own virtue and honor, still convinced that no living man could make him back down. He lived up to his legend.

El Paso was not happy to see him. Somewhat embarrassed by its reputation as a six-shooter capital, the town had undergone a temporary spasm of righteousness. A reform-minded administration had been voted

[12] Hardin, *Autobiography*, p. 121.

into office, and Jeff Milton had been imported from Arizona to take the job of chief of police. He had proved extraordinarily effective, but El Paso did not want anybody to rock the boat. Wes was thus regarded as a threat to the status quo, and on April 2 the *Times* noted, for his benefit, that "the day for man killers in El Paso has passed." About the same time Chief Milton called on Hardin and, according to his own story, made him take off his pistol.[13] The episode evidently became the subject of barroom discussion, and Hardin felt that a statement from him was called for. It appeared in the "On the Fly" column in the *Times* on April 17, and read in part: "Young Hardin, having a reputation for being a man who never took water, was picked out by every bad man who wanted to make a reputation, and there is where the 'bad men' made a mistake, for the young Westerner still survives many warm and tragic encounters." Now, the article continued, Hardin is "a quiet, dignified, peaceable man of business . . . but underneath the modest dignity is a firmness that never yields except to reason and law."

Wes had indeed become an El Paso businessman. When Miller's case was postponed until the following November, he rented an office in the First National Bank Building and made a valiant effort to establish

[13] J. Evetts Haley, *Jeff Milton: A Good Man with a Gun* (Norman: University of Oklahoma Press, 1948), p. 228.

himself in the practice of law. Very little legal business came in, however, perhaps because potential clients shied away from a lawyer who could be dangerous. With time on his hands, Wes spent more and more of his hours in saloons.

Another diversion became available to him on May 1, a month after his arrival. El Paso could not remain pure for very long, and on April 9 the citizens voted the reform administration out. Ed Fink replaced Jeff Milton as chief of police, and on the first of May a number of gambling rooms opened cautiously for business. Wes was among those who attended a poker session at the Acme. In the course of the evening he objected to the way the game was being run, took his money out of the pot, and walked out unmolested. The next night he did it again in a crap session at the Gem and invited anybody who did not like his play to step up and "show his manhood." He replied to actual and potential critics in another newspaper piece, explaining that the dealer had "grossly insulted" him.[14]

The two gambling houses filed suit, but his standing among his peers was seemingly not impaired. Misfortune was approaching, however, in the person of

[14] *El Paso Times*, May 14, 1895; C. L. Sonnichsen, *Pass of the North* (El Paso: Texas Western Press, 1968), pp. 327–329; John Middagh, *Frontier Newspaper* (El Paso: Texas Western Press, 1958), p. 66.

Mrs. Beulah Morose, companion and confidante of one
Martin Morose, a bad man from Eddy (now Carlsbad),
New Mexico, who had got away ahead of a charge of cattle theft and was hiding out across the river in Juarez.
Beulah stayed in El Paso, riding herd on most of Martin's bankroll. She roomed at Mrs. Herndon's boarding
establishment on Overland Street, where Wes also
found quarters. Beulah asked Wes to do what he could
for Martin and Wes agreed, but he soon became more
interested in doing what he could for Beulah. Word
went round that they were living together. Morose and
his friends heard about it and were understandably unhappy. There were threats and confrontations in Juarez, but nobody got hurt.[15]

All this time something was going on in El Paso
among ex-police chief Milton, Deputy U.S. Marshal
George Scarborough, Constable John Selman, and, in
all probability, John Wesley Hardin. There was a $500
reward out for Martin. The problem was to get him
back to El Paso. The upshot was the death of Morose,
who was ambushed as he tried to cross the railroad
bridge between the two towns. He may have been carry-
ing a considerable sum of money, and that money may
have found its way into Hardin's pocket. There may
have been hard feelings when Wes refused to divide.

[15] *El Paso Times*, April 24, 1895.

John Selman complained about it to saloonkeeper George Look and said in conclusion, "He has to come across or I'll kill him."[16]

Just before midnight on August 19, 1895, Selman did kill him. Hardin was rolling dice at the bar of the Acme when the constable came through the swinging doors and shot him in the head. Opinions still differ as to whether the bullet entered in front or in the back. Either way, Nagley's Undertaking Parlor took charge, conducting the funeral two days later and the burial in Concordia Cemetery not far from the grave of Martin Morose and not much farther from the spot where John Selman was later deposited. And there John Wesley Hardin lies today.

As this portion of the cemetery filled up and new areas were opened, the older graves were neglected and finally abandoned by the caretakers. Old Concordia became an eyesore and remained that way until the city built a wall around it in 1958 to keep it from public view. A few pioneers knew where Hardin rested, but there was no marker, no mound, no identifying feature at all, and the caretakers of the cemetery wanted to keep the location secret. Their experience with vandals and souvenir hunters convinced them that if anybody

[16] George Look, "Reminiscences" (manuscript), copy in possession of Wyndham K. White; Leon Metz, *John Selman, Texas Gunfighter* (New York: Hastings House, 1966), p. 178.

ever found that grave, Hardin would be in danger of removal, bone by bone.

I came into the picture in the 1940's. Following the trail of Texas feuds, I found myself tracing the footsteps of Wes Hardin, who had been involved on the side of the Taylors in the thirty-year Sutton-Taylor trouble. On a sultry day in July, 1943, I stopped in the little town of Smiley, Texas, where Hardin's grand-daughter lived with her husband Elmer Spellman. El-mer was big and serious with an eye which said that no liberties were to be taken with him, but he was a kindly man, and he and his quiet wife were gentlefolk in the best sense of the word. They talked with me about the Hardins and gave me an introduction to "Aunt Mattie" Smith of Fort Worth, John Wesley's sister, who told me more. I learned, among other things, that the family had long wanted to place a marker on the grave in El Paso. I promised to look into the matter when I got home.

I did so, and ran into a real hornets' nest. When I called on Mr. William R. Walker, the caretaker, in his office, he was aggressively hostile. He seemed to have a real obsession about the Hardin grave. The cemetery, he said, was constantly harassed by vandals who would destroy anything for the sake of a souvenir. People were constantly inquiring about the Hardin grave, but they got no help from him. While he lived, the location would not be revealed. He felt that I was interfering in his business, and he suggested that I walk out and stay out. By the time he finished, I was as upset as he was, and our angry voices could have been heard some distance away. Later I heard that he kept a pistol in his desk, and I was surprised and relieved that he hadn't used it.

Though I pursued the matter with some persistence, I found that there was nothing I could do while he was in charge. Even his brother-in-law A. B. Poe of the Poe Motor Company, who owned the cemetery and was a man of property and power in El Paso, said he could not help me. Mr. Walker was too much even for him. As a result, nothing more was done for fifteen years.

The curtain for the next act was raised by the late Lewis Nordyke of Amarillo, a journalist and free-lance historian. He decided to write a biography of John Wesley Hardin and asked what I could do to help. I put him in touch with the Spellmans, and they established a good relationship. Mrs. Spellman died in 1957 as quietly as she had lived, but Elmer continued to represent the family. The idea of burying Wes beside his wife came up, and on April 8, 1958, Nordyke wrote to Spellman: "I'd still like to see the family move the remains of Wes Hardin to the grave of Jane. I see no reason why the cemetery people at El Paso should be so

secretive about a man's grave." The letter reminded
Elmer of our abortive attempt to put up a marker in
1934. On May 1 he sat down and wrote me a letter
about it:

As you know, we have wanted for years to mark this grave,
but just never did get around to it. I have been wondering
if you knew the location of the grave. You remember that
you looked into the matter years ago and ran into trouble
with the caretaker. We have just about decided that owing
to the condition of the cemetery that perhaps we had better
bring him back and bury him by Jane. If you think we can
find the right grave and get by without a lot of publicity, I
would like to come out some time next month and bring
him back. We could put whatever is left in a chest that
would fit in the back of a station wagon and we can get by
on this end of the line without any fanfare or publicity.
Please write and tell me what you think.

I discussed this letter with two men who were interested in Hardin, and the result was the formation of
an informal but active John Wesley Hardin Commemorative Association with three members: Dr. S. D.
Myres of the history faculty of Texas Western College,
a seasoned historian and editor; Landon C. Martin, an
energetic drug salesman and history buff; and myself.
We agreed that Hardin's grave ought to be marked,
and we met repeatedly to discuss ways and means. One
possibility was to move the body back to the Asher
Cemetery near Coon Hollow in "the Sandies," where
Wes's wife Jane was buried. Martin thought we ought
to put him in a metal box and install him, with ap-

propriate inscription, in the wall of the county court-house, then being remodeled. He would thus be con-stantly in the public eye and might be of as much interest to the present generation as he had been to his own. Martin reminded us that a similar honor had been extended to King Fisher in a county farther east.

These alternatives were still under discussion when Mr. Spellman arrived on July 30, 1959. He brought with him Mr. and Mrs. W. N. Corder of Robs-town, Texas, and their small daughter Caroline. Mr. Corder was a six-foot-five-inch high-school superin-tendent. Mrs. Corder was John Wesley Hardin's great-granddaughter. They seemed like the best kind of Tex-as people, and thus the best kind of people anywhere.

By this time the belligerent and intransigent Mr. Walker had retired and moved to a house directly across the street from the cemetery headquarters. We suspected that he had positioned himself so he could intimidate Mr. Tom Dooley, the new caretaker, and see that nobody got to Wes Hardin's grave. Dooley was almost as obsessed as his predecessor. We met him on the morning of July 31, 1959. He was a short, dark, worried-looking fellow in khakis with a red face, a hook nose, and a watery eye, the result of seeking relief from his burdens at Tony's bar a few steps away. He came out on his porch to see what we wanted. Mr. Spellman told him.

At first Tom played dumb. "That was a long time

ago," he said. "There aren't any records, and I would have no way of locating the grave." Then he began on the consequences that would follow if a marker were put up. The stone would not last two weeks. It would be chipped away and maybe removed altogether. He couldn't be responsible for all that vandalism. He couldn't kill all the vandals. It had been the policy for fifty years not to reveal the location of the graves of such people. He had promised to keep it that way (we knew to whom). If he stopped being cautious, "they" could tear the cemetery to pieces. "I'll tell you the truth," he would say; "I'll be honest with you . . ." And the poor fellow would go off on another flight. I never saw a man suffer more. He worked himself up into a terrible state.[17]

He admitted that if the family demanded it, he would have to do what they said, but he hoped they wouldn't urge him. "I knew this would happen some day," he said mournfully, "but I hoped it wouldn't be while I was here."

He brightened up when Mr. Spellman remarked that the family had some idea of moving the body to East Texas. Yes, they could locate it and be absolutely sure of getting the right one. He had records going back to 1876 and complete records from 1885. They

[17] Sonnichsen notes, Hardin file.

were locked up in a steel safe, but he was doing ex-humations all the time and could guarantee that the job would be well done. All that was necessary was to get one of the forms from a mortician, send it off to Austin with the necessary signatures, wait for it to be approved, and then go ahead.

"Well," said Mr. Spellman, with some asperity, "if you can find the grave, you can show it to us—now. That's part of what we came for."

Realizing that he had overplayed his hand, Mr. Dooley changed his tactics. "I'll tell you what I'll do," he said. "If you will promise me that you won't put up a marker, I'll try to find it."

"I can't do that," Mr. Spellman told him. "I would have to consult the other descendants."

At that moment Dooley was called to the tele-phone. "Somebody stole a big faucet last night," he told us as he departed in haste, "and when the men turned on the water, they flooded the street."

Half an hour later he walked in without a word and went into a little office off the living room where we could hear him talking to himself, groaning and grumb-ling, "Well, I don't know . . ." Finally he appeared with a little rolled-up map and a piece of yellowed paper.

"I'll see if I can find it," he mumbled, obviously suffering from inward turmoil.

"It's too far to walk," he said as we left the house.

"Is this your car?" So we all got in and I drove the party to the abandoned part of the cemetery and we stood around and waited while he located landmarks and measured distances, all the time lecturing on his favorite subject.

"In this dry earth," he confided, "bodies stay well preserved. If they bury them six feet down, the water doesn't get to 'em. I dig up lots of people and there is always plenty left."

Finally he started from a particular tombstone, one of the few to be seen, looked right and left to establish rows, took half a dozen steps, and made a big cross on the ground. "This is within a foot or two of it," he said. "A man came to me a week or two ago and offered me a hundred dollars to show him this spot so he could take a picture."

"And I didn't even bring my camera," said Mrs. Corder, wryly.

This concluded our business, and we returned Mr. Dooley to his quarters. He was still in considerable distress and hardly took leave of us. He did say that if the grave were marked, he would recommend putting down a concrete slab and attaching the marker to it so firmly that a jackhammer would be needed to get it off. "They will take anything," he warned us, "and then dig into the grave and see if they can find anything there—including bones." Then he almost ran into the house.

Mr. Spellman went off for a visit to the Big Bend, confident that there would be no further problems. He underestimated Mr. Dooley, who had lost the battle but not the war and was about to begin a series of delaying actions which nearly defeated us.

On August 16 Elmer wrote that he had consulted with the other grandchildren and "it has been finally decided that the body will not be removed from its original and present resting place." Then he added: "This will be your authorization to erect a marker over the grave of John Wesley Hardin. Please contact Dr. Myres and Mr. Martin and proceed with the erection of the marker as discussed and agreed upon by us in the event the Grand Children decided that the body should not be moved."

Our first thought was to get Dave Crockett, an old and reputable contractor whom we all knew, to do the work. Dave was willing, and said he would do it at no charge for the sake of El Paso history. Then he had a change of heart, and we approached Mr. Dooley. On October 1 I wrote to Mr. Spellman:

You ask about our decision to let Dooley do the concrete work on the JWH marker. The decision was more or less taken out of our hands. Mr. Martin's friend Dave Crockett had promised to do the job free of charge but when it came time for us to move, he backed out. He said he has had many dealings with Mr. Walker in the past and might have more in the future and doesn't want to get into a hassle with him.

All three of us thought it would be just as well to turn the whole job over to Mr. Dooley. . . .
We were left without much recourse when he said he wanted to write to you about it. . . . If you don't hear from him within a week or ten days, let me know and I will go out and twist his arm.

Dooley never wrote. The months went by, and it became clear that he did not mean to write. On March 9, 1960, I commented to Mr. Spellman: "I am not surprised to hear that Mr. Dooley hasn't written to you. I thought he might, but he was too involved emotionally in the business to be very reliable." I added that we were thinking about asking the El Paso County Historical Society to take the matter up and assume responsibility for marking the grave. They might sponsor a reburial at another El Paso cemetery.

John Neff, then president of the society, was interested. He asked Colonel Albion Smith (U.S.A., Retired) to organize a committee to consider the matter, and the colonel called to ask me to be one of the group.[18] I said I would, and he promised to get me an invitation to the next meeting of the executive committee of the society so I could present my case.

The executive committee met for lunch and business at Hotel Paso del Norte on April 26, 1960. Colonel Smith introduced me. I sketched the background of the Hardin affair and read Mr. Spellman's letter in which

[18] Colonel Albion Smith, April 1, 1960, telephone interview.

he expressed his willingness to let the society handle the matter. My note on what came next reads as follows:

After my presentation the fireworks started. Mrs. Enrique Flores and Mrs. Harry Varner were terribly opposed. They felt that this was a bad man and that the Society should not honor him.

Dr. Eugene Porter said he didn't think we had to honor him. We could put on the marker, "This is where the SOB lies."

Mrs. Flores said that while there were all these fine citizens whom we hadn't honored, she couldn't bear to have anything done for such a man.

President Neff remarked that it was true people like Juan Hart had done much to build the town, but tourists never asked to see the grave of Juan Hart.

I told them I thought we had no right to pass moral judgments in a matter like this. The man was famous—had killed over thirty men (a great distinction, said Mrs. Flores) and that people all over the world were curious about him. They ought to know that he was a two-sided character. He never saw anything bad in what he did—was superintendent of the prison Sunday school, etc.

Chris Fox, ex-sheriff and PR man at the State National Bank, made a sensible little talk in which he disclaimed admiration for Billy the Kid, John Wesley Hardin, *et al.*, but said we couldn't argue that they were not of historical interest. He thought we ought to do something about the grave. Mrs. Flores and Mrs. Varner shook their heads violently.

I said that although I knew of two of the members who would stay away, I could see quite a ceremony at a reburial—national publicity—maybe a photographer from *Life* (Mrs. Varner and Mrs. Flores thought that would be awful).

Finally President Neff said he thought the Society

ought to declare itself for or against keeping Colonel Smith's committee going. A vote was taken and the ayes had it. Mrs. Flores and Mrs. Varner dissented and asked that their votes be recorded.

Then Otis Coles of Coles Brothers Realty, a real old-timer, got up and said he thought he was the only living El Pasoan who had known John Wesley Hardin and his advice was, DON'T DISTURB HIM.

The meeting adjourned and I made my peace as best I could with Mrs. Flores and Mrs. Varner, both of whom I loved. Mrs. Flores said there was nothing personal in her stand.

At the door retired U.S. Army Major Dick McMasters stopped me and said he had an idea: put a plaque on the wall of the cemetery saying, "Near this spot in an unmarked grave . . ." I said it might turn out to be the only way. Albion Smith said he would call a committee meeting soon, and Otis Coles had an anecdote about a friend of his who had worked as a clerk at the Pierson Hotel and got in bad with John Wesley Hardin. Hardin said this man had not treated one of his friends right and announced that he was looking for him. Coles scrambled around fast to get to his friend before it was too late, found him, and persuaded him to get out of town. He went back to Indiana and stayed there.

Colonel Smith made the next move. On May 1 he called me and said he favored placing the marker on the cemetery wall. "I don't want to get into this thing

too far," he said, and went on to point out that the society was "a talking society and not an acting society."
"When the vote was taken at our meeting, only seven
people voted to keep the committee. The rest kept their
hands in their laps. They always get some sucker like
me who *will* do something, and if things go wrong, I
get the blame."

When he asked me for my recommendation, I said
I favored moving the body to some place where the
grave could be cared for—a move which would need a
court order.

"I don't want to get mixed up in any legal shenani-
gans," he said.

"A court order will be necessary," I reminded him,
"no matter where the body is taken, or by whom. But if
Tom Dooley could be convinced that we would go that
far, he would probably make no further objections to
marking the grave. Elmer Spellman will come out again
if there is any prospect for real action."

"Why," Smith demanded somewhat plaintively,
"if the family wants something done, don't they do it
themselves?"

"They tried once," I reminded him, "and nothing
happened."

The colonel shook his head sadly. He obviously
felt that he was holding a potato which might become
hot and wished he could drop it. He promised, how-

ever, that he would confer further with President Neff.

The result was a letter, dated May 2, to Neff, with a copy for me. Smith proposed that we choose between two plans: a bronze marker on the wall at Concordia Cemetery, or a marker at the grave, if the site could be determined. He cited advantages and disadvantages of both plans. Among the disadvantages of Plan Two were the "hostile attitude, already known to exist, on the part of the custodian of the cemetery," the need for a court order, and the fact that a marker "would assist vandals seeking to disturb the grave." He preferred Plan One.

Neither plan was adopted. In cases like this where there is a division of opinion, the easiest thing to do is to do nothing, and that is just what the historical society did.

The effort, however, did bear some fruit. The grave remained unmarked, but a marker was placed on the building in which John Wesley Hardin died. Chris Fox's State National Bank, largely at Mr. Fox's behest, had embarked on a program of placing bronze markers at historic points in El Paso, and in November, 1962, the bank unveiled a plaque attached to the wall of Lerner's ladies-ready-to-wear store on the site of the Acme Saloon, where Hardin rolled dice for the last time. The build-up was impressive—newspaper publicity, television interviews, invitations. The ceremonies began at noon on November 19. A fine rain was falling, but a rather large crowd had assembled, including visiting celebrities and home-town pioneers. Sheriff "Dogie" Wright of Sierra Blanca was there (his grandfather had been a participant in the Sutton-Taylor feud). Mrs. W. D. Howe was there. Her husband had been a justice of the peace in 1895 and had conducted the hearing for John Selman. Jane Burges Perrenot was there. Her father had been a young El Paso lawyer, recently arrived, at the time of the shooting. Mr. and Mrs. Joe Clements of Carlsbad were there. The Hardins and the Clementses were cousins, and Joe as a small boy had gone hunting with Wes Hardin. Mayor Ralph Seitsinger was there, as were George Matkin (president) and Hal Daugherty (top vice-president) of the State National Bank. Chris Fox took charge and told us why we were assembled. At the conclusion of his remarks Lieutenant Jim Parks of the El Paso Police Department, on signal from the speaker, cut loose with three resounding pistol shots which startled the assemblage according to plan.[19] When it was over, a select group of dignitaries enjoyed a steak-sandwich lunch at the International Club at the bank's expense, and that concluded the celebration.

I could not help wondering what Wes Hardin's

[19] *El Paso Times*, November 2, 1962.

feelings would have been had he been present. He would probably have been puzzled and incredulous. Most of the people involved did not really know what we were commemorating, and the curious bystanders must have been completely in the dark. The only really intelligent reaction that I heard came from Conrey Bryson of KTSM. He said he had a program coming up in which he intended to make the point that we all like direct action and envy a man who had the nerve to pull his gun and settle his problems once and for all. I felt that the idea made sense.

Futile though the gesture may have been, it was the best we could do for the moment, and nothing more was attempted in Hardin's behalf for three years. Then the family decided to try again. Elmer Spellman called me from his home in Burnet and said the descendants wanted to go ahead with marking the grave, even if it took a supreme effort. It would be my job to find somebody who could and would do it.

"We want a marker with only Hardin's name on it," he said, "with dates, set in a heavy slab of concrete. Jane's stone is that way, and the grandchildren say, 'The simpler the better.' "[20]

I mentioned a story, which was coming out of Tony's bar, where Mr. Dooley sometimes became elo-

[20] E. D. Spellman, July 14, 1968, (telephone interview).

quent over his beer, that one of the Hardin descendants had got a court order to stop all proceedings. Mr. Spellman was amused at that. He was in touch with all the descendants, he said, and they wanted the marker installed. About September 1 he planned to come to El Paso himself to make sure the job was done. In the meantime, would I look for somebody who could and would do it? I said I would. We discussed the fact that Mr. Walker had passed on, leaving Mr. Dooley under considerably less pressure. The result was a commission to Mr. Narzinsky of the Pioneer Monument Company, conveyed in a letter to me, "to erect a marker of Georgia gray granite over the grave of John Wesley Hardin, located in Concordia Cemetery, El Paso, Texas."[21] A check accompanied the authorization, to be delivered when the monument was in place.

Mr. Dooley made one last attempt to halt the proceedings. He told Mr. Narzinsky he could not come in without a court order, and Mr. Narzinsky called me. "Tell Tom Dooley," I said, "that we are going ahead, and he might as well give in. The court order will be forthcoming if we have to get Mr. Spellman out here to apply for it."[22]

That took care of the caretaker, and on Friday,

[21] E. D. Spellman to Pioneer Monument Company, September 16, 1965, copy to C. L. Sonnichsen.

[22] Sonnichsen notes, September 20, 21, 1965, Hardin file.

September 24, 1965, the work began. Five days later Mr. Narzinsky and I made our final inspection. As we walked up to the grave, Mr. Dooley appeared in his pickup for a final interview, straw hat, khaki pants, red face, watery eyes, and all. I trained my camera on him, and he shied off at once. "I don't want to get in on anything like that," he protested, but he seemed to be in a good mood. "I had the grave located in three books," he told us. "I bet I have had 500 cousins and relatives of his out here looking for that grave. Some of those people would dig it up looking for a pistol or something. When Mr. Walker turned the cemetery over to me, he said, 'There is one thing I want to tell you. I swore years ago, and the man I took over from swore [here Mr. Dooley put his hands together as if in prayer], and I want you to swear that you will never reveal the location of that grave. If you do, they'll tear up your cemetery.' "

Both of us assured him that we hadn't told anybody about the marker—and that neither of us was going to talk.

"Chris Fox called me," he said. "He had heard a rumor. I told him I couldn't say a word until something was laid down. I wish you would let Chris know, but nobody else."

I promised I would call Mr. Fox at the State National Bank (and I did later). As we were getting ready to break up, I said to Dooley, "I hope we can be friends now," and to Narzinsky, "Tom doesn't have a very good opinion of me."

"It wasn't you," Dooley protested. "It was that fellow with the black, curly hair" (meaning Landon C. Martin of our commemorative committee, who may have seemed a little persistent). He then launched into an account of "that policeman," meaning Leon C. Metz, who was getting ready to write his book on John Selman and had brought Selman's granddaughter out to the cemetery to look for the grave.

"He threatened to put me in jail if I didn't dig up the records on Selman. I went over every record we had here, and there was nothing on him."

His last words to me, just before he drove off—the last words I ever heard him speak—were, "Yes, we're friends." Not long afterward he went to the hospital, and the doctors found gangrene and blood clots inside him. I hope we were not even partly responsible. We were glad to hear that he had recovered, retired, and moved to Farmington, New Mexico.

On October 14 I sent snapshots of the marker to Mr. Spellman with the remark, "Here is the evidence!"

There is a postscript. Marshal Hail, staff writer for the *El Paso Herald-Post*, got wind of the transaction four months after the event, and on February 25, 1966, he ran a feature story in his newspaper with a picture of

John Wesley Hardin and another of Mr. Narzinsky pointing to his handiwork. By this time Bob Narzinsky, Walter's son, was in charge at the cemetery, and he brought a new deal to Old Concordia. Many people in the course of a year make pilgrimage to Hardin's tomb, but nobody has disturbed the grave.

"Since I seem to have status as the El Paso gunfighter authority," says Leon Metz, "everybody in town refers queries about the grave to me. I average three or four phone calls a month and maybe a couple of letters. One lady got me out of bed at five-thirty on a Sunday morning—said she was a tourist on her way through and wanted to see the grave."

"In my judgment," he adds, "Hardin's grave is the top tourist attraction. And it could be better exploited. We have the only *genuine* Boot Hill in the country."[23]

So the pilgrims are coming to the shrine, but not a one of them will ever know what it cost in time, travel, hope deferred, and emotional stress to put that monument where it is today and where, one hopes, it will remain for the foreseeable future.

[23] Leon C. Metz to C. L. Sonnichsen, February 2, 1977.